AF410836

NOW. OR NEVER.

FUCK IT!

TANIA WINTHER

Copyright © 2026 by Tania Winther

Title: *Now. Or Never. FUCK IT.*

ISBN: 979-8-89965-984-3

Cover design: Bodil Mostad Olsen
Publisher: Midnight Sun Press
Printed by: Ingram Spark

Original photographer of cover photo: Keduri Williams
Model: Mini

All rights reserved.
No part of this publication may be reproduced, stored in a retrieval system, or transmitted in any form or by any means electronic, mechanical, photocopying, recording, or otherwise without the prior written permission of the author.

My Wildfire" has also found life as a song through a musical collaboration with Australian singer and musician Geoff Healey, and can be found on Spotify, Apple Music, and other streaming platforms.

To be strong is not to never fall, but to rise each time you do.

-T.

This collection is for you
to understand that

you don't have to be strong all the time.

It is a book about being human,
and about being brave enough to feel.

A QUIET BEGINNING

I didn't know where my voice was. Not until I lost everything that kept it held down. This book was not planned. It pushed its way forward, like a cry from a place I had long forgotten.
The poetry collection itself is the result of

several years of exploration and searching for myself. A journey to find my way back to who I am.

It pushed its way forward, like a cry from a place I had long forgotten, or perhaps did not want to answer.

The poems are not perfect.
They are simply true.
True to me.
Perhaps also to you.

You don't need to have all the answers.
You only need to begin.

For the past six years, I have devoted myself to one
thing:
finding my way back to myself.
Through what was torn away.
Through what disappeared into silence, grief, and
collapse.
Through what could not be saved.

This is not a collection of poems written to impress.
They were written to survive.

Words, art, and creativity became my way of

breathing
when everything else stopped making sense.

When I no longer knew who I was
without all the roles I had carried.

These are the traces of a process,
a quiet rebellion,
a path home.

If you recognize yourself here,
you are not alone.
-T.

Sometimes you have to lose everything to find yourself.
-T.

Now or Never - Fuck It

I have waited
as if life were something that had to approve me
first
as if someone sat somewhere
with a form
and a stamp
and wrote
you may begin now

but no letter ever came

only days that looked the same
only thoughts going in circles
only that voice whispering

soon

soon

soon

I'm tired of soon
tired of standing on the threshold of my own life
like a guest
who doesn't want to impose
who doesn't want to make noise
who doesn't want to be seen too much

but I am here
I am fucking here
what am I waiting for?

a better version of myself?
a less frightened body?
a clearer language?
a day when everything makes sense?

that day does not exist
that day is a lie
a pretty, well-behaved lie
we tell ourselves
so we can avoid beginning

so fuck it

fuck what isn't perfect
fuck what isn't clear
fuck what isn't finished
fuck what isn't understood

I'm beginning anyway

I write with what is left
with what trembles
with what has no words yet
with what has been silent far too long

I write because I have to
not because I am ready

maybe it will be ugly

maybe it will be wrong
maybe nobody will understand a damn thing

but it is mine
and it exists
and that is more than nothing

so this is it

not the beginning of something perfect
but the beginning of something true

not a finished voice
but one that dares to be heard

not a plan
but a kick in the direction of life

now or never

and I choose now

even though my hands are shaking
even though I doubt
even though I do not know

I choose now

because if not
who the fuck is going to do it for me?

I
waited for courage
found
only unrest
used
it anyway

sometimes "fuck it"
is the most honest thing.
-T.

Like Mirrors and Moments

I am never in the same shape twice.
Light hits me and refracts
each movement becomes a new version of me,
turned forward
by the angle of your gaze.
You try to define me
as if I were
one color,
one pattern,
but I was born of mirrors
and moments.
What you see

depends entirely
on where you stand
and how gently
you turn.
Inside me,
nothing stands still.
Not sorrow. Not joy.
Not even the memories
of what just was.
I break
in beautiful ways.
Piece myself back together
in silence.
Fragments
of what I've survived
and what I'm becoming.
Not scattered,
but scattering
with purpose.

I am a kaleidoscope.

You are worthy of the warmth that meets you.
-T.

INVISIBLE ROOTS

There are roots claimed by no soil.
They float between worlds,
neither from here nor there,
searching for a land that remembers them.
They coil around the wind,
feed on forgotten memories,
and sing softly in the language of mist.
To exist is sometimes to drift.
To belong is a legend whispered to the stars.

Time doesn't always taste sweet,
but it carries with it the possibility to grow, even in the
dark.
-T

Your Scapegoat

You were the sun that warmed me
and the shadow that never let me breathe

Your hands gave me life
but also held me captive
in ways I could not escape
a safety that became a cage

I know your heart was full
overflowing with care
but there was always something there
an expectation

a need
unspoken in everything you did

You wrapped your love
in chains
and called it care

Every kind gesture
carried a silent demand
a weight I did not see
until I lay buried beneath it

You needed me
to be your mirror

So you shaped a version of me
that fit inside your world

You said I was weak
if I did not follow
if I did not bend
to the shape you carved out

Your love was always
a weapon

Guilt wrapped in warmth
guilt placed in my hands
disguised as tenderness

Every time I tried to breathe
you tightened your grip

I became the scapegoat
for your mistakes
your rage
your defeats

You painted me
as the problem
as the one who did not understand
how much you gave
how much you suffered

and in your eyes
I was always
the reason for the cracks
in your world

but I began to see

the mirror you held up before me
was shattered
distorted

it was not myself I saw
it was you

your insecurity
your unmet needs
your fear

you needed me to need you
to feel whole

but inside your need
I disappeared

but now I see

I am not your shadow
I am not the face
you wanted me to wear
I am not your scapegoat

I carry my own breath now
my own steps
my own name

and still
I love you

but I need more than your love now
I need space
to breathe
to break free from the weight
of what you never said
but always demanded

to find myself
the woman you never fully saw

now
I stand here
without your shape
without your voice
in my head

quieter now

I breathe
for the first time
without asking

I was your scapegoat
now I break free from the chains

I was your scapegoat
now it is my turn
to tear myself loose

I carried the guilt you gave me
now I lay it down.

I was reflected crookedly,
a story told
from a single angle.
-T.

Set Yourself Free

You gave too much
and slowly
you lost yourself.
Those who held your hand in the light
let it go in the dark.
But you
you were never empty.
You were simply divided
to fill others.

Now it's enough.

You are your own strength.
Don't hide anymore.
Stop that now.

*You cannot empty yourself
to fill others
who never ask if you need refilling.*
-T.

Every Day

Pat yourself on the shoulder
in front of the mirror.
You are here.
You're standing.
You carry everything you've been through
and still, you move forward.
You are brave.
You are strong.
You have survived.
Not everyone does.
And no one knows
how much it cost you
to get here.

Being patient with yourself is the bravest step.
-T.

Façade

Sometimes it hurts to hear others' truth about who
you are.
It can come harsh, cold, brutal.
But remember:
It's their gaze.
Their filters.
Their fear, perhaps.
It's not your truth.
You know yourself best.

Hold on to that.

*Not everyone who receives
thinks about what it cost you to give.*
-T.

Is That Why?

He is kind.
He only means well.
He opens the door
without asking for anything in return.

But my heart

stands still.
Have I been hurt so much
that I no longer
believe I deserve
what doesn't hurt?

It's okay to open the door,
to welcome the warm wind.
Kindness is not just for others
you also have the right to receive it.
-T.

CONFUSION

I don't know
if I'm moving forward
or just running in circles
inside myself.

Everything feels both right and wrong
at the same time.
Thoughts cross each other
like a large knot
I pull at one end,
but it only tightens.

I search for an answer
but the questions multiply
every time I blink.

What do I want?

What do I feel?

Where did I go
in the middle of all this?

Don't let others' silence become your own prison wall.
-T.

THE AFTERMATH

It happened.
But my body knows it before I do.
It closes like a book
that cannot bear to be read.

I move on,
but the ground beneath me
is not fully built.

People say:
"It's over now."
But no one sees

that it's still happening
inside me.

Every day.
In the sound of a door.
In empty rooms.
In my own breaths.

I'm learning to live
as if nothing was torn apart
while I gather the threads
that refuse to bind.

Moving on
is not forgetting
it's learning
to carry the weight
without letting it break you

every time you stand up again.

You cannot water every garden
with the blood from your own roots.
-T.

Outlet

It's okay to scream.
Okay to feel everything
all at once.
You can laugh
while the tears fall.
Cry
while your heart beats with relief.
There is no right way
to feel.
Only real.
Don't let anyone tell you
that you must quiet down,
calm down,
be ashamed.
The body knows.

The mind knows.
Something needs to come out.
Let it have space.
Let it breathe.
Let it be.

Vulnerability is not weakness; it is true strength in daring to feel.
-T.

Under The Surface

It's strange with facades.
How we think
we can read a person
from the outside.

A smile.

A tidy home.

A gathered family.

But we know better now.
Facades lie.
They are painted with duty,
polished with fear,
and hold on to what cannot withstand the light of
day.

Behind closed doors
are stories
we will never hear
if we don't listen
carefully.

Let the wounds breathe.
Let yourself heal
without hurry.
Healing has its own clock.
-T.

LISTEN

Please
listen.

To those who whisper in silence,
who do not dare to shout.
The unspoken lives
between the lines,
in the pauses,
in glances that do not meet.
There lies the truth
they do not dare to carry alone.

Don't wait for courage. Do it now,
fail, get up, fail again,
always rise again.
-T.

Too Many Years in Silence

I lost so many years
because I didn't dare.
Didn't dare to say it out loud,
didn't dare to open the door
to what was burning inside.
I would rather drown
in my own silence,
in my own fear.
Why did I let them
whip me into silence?

Why did I choose
to be trapped
in my own darkness?

Some flowers take longer
before they dare to turn toward the light.
You are one of them,
and that is beautiful.

-T.

Through Pitch Darkness

The revelation came quietly,
through the darkness.
I had to fall so deep
that I was caught
by shadows,
by machines,
by what was supposed to help me
breathe,
but held me tight.
There, in the blackness,

I learned to know myself again
between the silence and the sounds,
between fear and hope.

You won't get anywhere
with just thoughts and wishes.
You have to get up.
Walk.
Do.
-T.

Allowed To Feel

It's okay to feel fear.
Okay to say no.
Setting boundaries
is not weakness
it's taking care of yourself.
You don't always need to say yes
to be seen or to be loved.

A period is also a sentence.
Sometimes saying no is the bravest yes.
-T.

Trapped

Like a bird in a cage,
without the power to choose for yourself.
Not because you couldn't,
but because you said yes
to everything, always.
Made sure others were okay,
gave yourself away,
so they could have what they wanted.
But that is not a life worthy of you.

It's time to stop.
Stop being the cage.
Stop being silent.

Take back your freedom.

My voice is free,
not trapped in your mouth.
-T.

My Words

Don't swallow my words.
Don't put anything in my mouth.
I say what I want to say,
in my own way,
at my own pace.
Let me be my own voice,
let me own my truth.

*Don't wait for the right moment.
It is the action
that makes the moment right.*
-T.

Why Does it Cost so Much to Know Your Own Worth?

Sometimes life must be torn apart
for you to see yourself clearly.
Sometimes everything you thought you needed
must disappear
for you to discover

that the only thing you truly needed
was yourself.
It's unfair,
but maybe that's also where strength lives:
In the breaks.
In what was taken.
In what remained.
You.

It's okay to scream, cry and howl
when no one truly sees you.
-T.

HOWL YOURSELF FORWARD

When someone sees you,
and says:
You have been through too much
for too long.
Not been heard.
Not been seen.
Then it's okay
to scream.
To howl.
To let free what burns behind your ribs.

Brilliant in your own language.

-T.

My Galaxy Boy

You wake
and the world arrives too loud.
Too bright.
Too sudden.

And I watch
as you flinch at sunlight,
wrestle with your layers,
trip over words
that never quite land
where you want them to.

Your mind,
a galaxy I can't chart.
Your heart,
a song I know
but cannot sing back.

I hold you
while the storm moves through you,
and I hold you still
when you won't let me near.

Some days,
I am bone-tired
from translating the world
into something softer for you
and myself.

I ache
not because you are broken
you are not
but because the world
keeps trying to shatter you
for being different.

And loving you
this deep, deep love
is both the light
that saves me
and the weight
that presses into my chest
when I haven't slept
in days.

But then, my god
you smile,
and I remember.

Dedicated: For the beautifully different, and those who love them fiercely.

*No time to grieve for roses when the forests are
burning.*

- Juliusz Słowacki

My Wildfire

My Wildfire

You touched me and the forests inside me flared not gently,

not like a kiss,

but like the match that forgets it was ever small.

I burned not for ruin, but for release.

Even the stars watched from a distance

But you

You vanished in the blaze you lit inside me.

Chose the sharpest edge of silence and called it
peace.

Left your body like broken bark,

your name like smoke in my lungs.

And I,

I sift through ash, finding pieces of myself

you never meant to leave behind.

The fire is out.

But the ruins remember.

And damn you for dying like that, and leaving me to
live in what's left.

They said I should've known.
But how do you fear the fire
when it feels like coming home?
-T.

Where The Fire Ends

I used to think
love was supposed to hurt.
That heat meant depth,
and scars meant truth.

But now
now I see the quiet things.
The way peace feels
like an open window
instead of a wildfire at the door.

You weren't the end of me,

though you tried.
You were the end
of who I thought I had to be
to feel wanted.

I still carry smoke
in my lungs,
but I breathe softer now.

There is life
where the fire ends.
Green things growing
through what's left of me.
And not everything
needs to burn
to feel alive.

-T.

I swear
if I ever see your ghost
in the smoke again,
I will not reach for it.

I will not water it.
I will not weep.
I will simply walk away
glowing.
-T.

Storms Come Without Warning

It's okay to feel exhaustion.
Life is not always clear.
Some days the wind is gentle,
as if everything makes sense.
Other days
the storm comes without warning
and you stand there,
soaking wet
and trembling,

with no idea
what hit you.
That doesn't mean you are weak.
It simply means
that you are human.

Between the words I did not say,
I find my voice.

-T.

Tanianian Time

I've never been one to trust the hands of the clock.
My pace is calm, rooted in the belief that time is not
an enemy, but a companion
one who dances to its own rhythm,
never bound to anyone else's agenda.
I call it Tanianian time
an art of waiting,
of trusting that things unfold
when they're meant to,
not when we demand it.

Even though I'm a workaholic,

I know that in this flow,
things get done
sometimes more than most would expect.
I may not follow the world's familiar beat,
but I finish with precision, dedication, and passion
not just in time,
but in my own way.

I don't measure time in deadlines or lost minutes.
I find joy in the in-betweens
in the breath before the next step,
in the pause before the shift.
For every second holds its own magic,
and I refuse to rush past it.

In the stillness of this timing,
I understand that I am neither late nor early
I am simply present.
And that is enough.

PS: I dedicate this to you P.H.D.

I stayed.
I listened.
I awakened to myself.
-T.

The Slow Return

There was a time I forgot how to move.

How to speak without apology. How to name myself without shrinking.

I disappeared without anyone noticing.

Not all at once but slowly, like a tide retreating, so far out you forget it was ever there.

I lived underground.

Not in death, but in pause.

Held in the hush

of becoming something

I didn't yet have words for.

There was no light there,

only the feeling that something might grow if I
stayed long enough.

I didn't bloom.

I didn't rise.

I stayed.

I listened.

I let the silence do what it needed to.

Now, I begin again. Not with certainty,

but with softness.

A step.

A breath.

A name I am learning to say without fear. This is not the end of sorrow.

But it is the beginning of me.

My rebirth.

It takes time to find your way home to yourself.
Don't give up the journey.
-T.

www.ingramcontent.com/pod-product-compliance
Lightning Source LLC
Chambersburg PA
CBHW020457160726
47991CB00007B/2693